Jason Waddle is graduating with a B.A. in English literature from McMaster University. Jason has also studied Psychology at Concordia University. He has published multiple poems and short stories. He is a full-time writer who has built a life with his wife and son in Ontario, Canada.

For my son, Jonathan Waddle, and in memory of Bruce Waddle.

Jason Waddle

AWAKE IN DREAMS, SLEEPING DEATH AWAY

AUSTIN MACAULEY PUBLISHERS™

LONDON • CAMBRIDGE • NEW YORK • SHARJAH

Ordering Information:
Quantity sales: special discounts are available on quantity purchases by corporations, associations, and others. For details, contact the publisher at the address below.

Publisher's Cataloging-in-Publication data
Waddle, Jason
Awake in Dreams, Sleeping Death Away

ISBN 9781645755173 (Paperback)
ISBN 9781645755180 (Hardback)
ISBN 9781645755197 (ePub e-book)

Library of Congress Control Number: 2020900743

www.austinmacauley.com/us

First Published (2020)
Austin Macauley Publishers LLC
40 Wall Street, 28th Floor
New York, NY 10005
USA

mail-usa@austinmacauley.com
+1 (646) 5125767

Special thanks to Fr. Gary Schlack, my wife Jenny, Cornelia Seckel, Raymond J. Steiner, Professor Jeffery Donaldson, Iris Zapach, and the entire English Department at McMaster University.

"O God, I could be bounded in a nutshell and count myself a king of infinite space—were it not that I have bad dreams."

-Hamlet 2.2.254-56

Author's Note:

Some of the poems in 'Awake in Dreams, Sleeping Death Away' were previously published in the following magazines:

Poems published in Arttimes Journal:

"Big City"

"Does it Really Matter"

"Ageless Fun"

"Mastery"

"The End"

"Shakespeare's Comedic Theme?"

Poem published in Floyd County Moonshine:

"Bookshelf"

A Child's Day

You have played with
Magical friends in the air
And you have created
Unicorns and dragons fair
But the night's chandelier
Being the all night
Night-light…the moon:
It's bed time
Get tucked in not too tight.
The day's play
Now out of sight, yet
In the mind you dream
Of unicorns and dragons tonight.
Tomorrow enters your room
And sees you
Army crawl out of bed
And unto the floor
And out the door…
What new friends does your
Imagination has in store?

Big City

Curious to see
The homeless
Feeding birds…!
Last sliver of bread and
Glimpses of kindness unsaid
So peek in why not
Contrastingly
At the well-to-do
Spoils:
Yet! Never enough to chew.
Lips that drip
Of wine
Elegant cars
And not a dime
Nor the time
To ponder or wonder
About the souls
Lost in pockets
Of city beats:
The cold and hungry wearing
The government's streets.

Black Dog Barking

The one dog I owned
And one that owns me
That faithful German Shepard
Oh, fateful other

Gentle, obedient, and loving since puppyhood
Choking, smothering, spirit-killing bark
My Shepard sits by my soaking soul
Oh, black dog barking-raining on me...

Baily
A name good enough for any Shepard
Yet you were no ordinary dog
You acted as a guardian
Protecting what you loved...
Oh other

There are many names for you
Though none really fit the pain you cause
Yes, you are faithful too
Never leaving me alone

Now that Baily has passed
You sit taller
A taunting Intimidating
Black dog barking.

Bookshelf

Are books on a shelf
Silent or alive?
I'd argue it's one large
Living organism
Involved in a conversation
With itself
Yet not by itself
And not talking only
To itself
All books are in discourse
With every other book
On the shelf.
In fact
The books converse
With books all around the World:
They debate
They agree
To disagree
And sometimes just agree
On facts
And that's no fiction!
Each book Shut tight and

Temporarily confined
Within the bind
Of its fold
So untold is a truth told
Kept secret
In a book
For a reader to inherit.

Shadows

Copycat shadow
Mimicking motions perfectly
A rip off of the original how
It stings to see another as good as me.
Follower of my ways
Creeper of night and sunlight
Stalker hovering over Mondays.
Running away works out not, yet
Shadows' blame received, but not exclusively.
They say all is in the head for me is blind
Short on rationality… I am locked inside this mind.
There he goes they say:
Stepping, stomping, swearing
At his shadow all week through Sunday.
Shadows.
It was thought they haunt him and
Not just follow, or copycat.
Haunt him it does.
Crazy, crazy, he was, and
Crazy, crazy that boy Jack will stay when
Running from shadows each and every day.
Till one bend in the day

Anna's shadow reached out
Reached out for her!
This town birth's crazy, no doubt, so
Shadows worked out their plans in dark
What was organized played out even in light.
Folks began crawling
On their knees with a bark, and
Tom the ex-barber says the moon hollers at him
Some disease that took the town by fright?
All went chasing down their shadows like crazy men, and
their shadows chased them.
Time sucks each back to their rooms
A call for bed time with a shout
To all on the ward: "Lights out."

Campsite

The smell of burning wood as
We walk off through patches
Of green. Birds are heard
Though unseen and nature's eye
Is beginning to moisten. Our
Once dry foot prints are
Now muddied up and each step is squishy wet.
Gone is the wood smell
And our way back we forget.

Catalogue of Sleep

What if you could put
The dreams of a single mind
In theatrical motion…?
In filing
And colligating them together
Putting them into
A compilation:
Flipping them at the finger tip
Like a flip Book.
Could we see them in silent
Action?
If So
You would be awake
For the first time
Watching yourself
Sleep.

Contradictions

The weather in life has taken its toll
I am dry and empty in my soul
Well-fed and still going hungry
Confused over which love
Has ever loved me.
Life is precarious
And curious little thing of
Constructed contradictions
Too big for contemplation is
This little thing.
Love is life, life is love
Two truths intertwined
And set on fire from above
In hearts
At times melting, and
Other times cold.
All these elements added up
Life tastes bold, but
Truth sweetens a kiss
Yet a lie makes ugly
The beautiful temptress.
The importance of love is not a harvest

Its maintenance cannot be taken for granted:
In this life love's importance is
What's been intentionally planted.

Down with the Ship

Gasping for air
Swallowing spaces of darkness
Unfound and anchored in vastness
Back and forth
Stumbling, falling
Swaying and sinking
Eyes stinging
Ears ringing
Grasping at bubbles
Desperate for air
Suffocating your thinking
Down, down, down…
And so too is the ship sinking
Midnight darkness
Sunken Sailor
Blessed Blackness
The ocean's breathless inhaler
Bubbles, bubbles, bubbles
Arms stretched
Lifeless limbs

A trail of bubbles
Sanding the Ocean's bottom
Relieved of a captain's troubles.

Devil's Advocate

You say you're playing devil's advocate
And I say you're just the devil though
Your eyes pretend gentle.
My eyes look away knowing enough
Not to test your metal.
You speak softly of the truth
Yet the words make it difficult to stand, and
Those who follow them fall down damned.
I am fooled not, so you are off to another
Unsuspecting sister or brother.
You'll be back with your baiting…
Temptation is what makes you Satan.

Divisions in Motion

Two paths bisect
By one tree middle
Equidistantly and having
No single authority over
Its own origins. People are
Peopling and passing through
The left and right sides.
Some stand back:
On pause, some vomit.
There is an authority
That naturally rules over
Them. This middle way
Is empty and absent of
All particular directional
Confrontation.
A simple divide
And split down the
Center which all
Time-travelers must
In line with.

The motion of movement
Moves the tree into
Vibrations which flow to
The left, the right.

Does It Really Matter?

Does it really matter
If life were nothing
But a downward ladder?
I guess it doesn't really matter.
Earth let me in so a life can begin
For some meaning is found
Tipping a bottle of gin
But I guess it doesn't really matter.
Now I've climbed to the top of the ladder
Only to look down the other way:
Now I know it doesn't really matter
For my downs have been my ups
And my ups have been my downs.
It really doesn't matter.
Time to get off this ladder with a frown
In need of a change of scenery
Oh, my luck, a merry-go-round.

Dirty Mind

Legs wide open…
Let's begin
With a sardonic smile
He pushed right in.
On top:
Hovering in his gaze…
Fingers pressing her buttons to amaze.
Sitting on a chair
Pushed into the crevasse of desk space
One's thoughts streaming from pure to dirty:
Spring time office cleaning
Before we open at the AM of 9:30.

Electrical Storm in the Eye

Wonder the thunder
And lightning
Streaking at night
Spiking like a Viking
Dressed like a dendrite
Awesome energy and power
Out on the porch watching
A fine electrical shower.

Awakened to the Dream

Deep in a dream I lay dreaming
Awake in my sleep
Watching memories streaming
Where's the switch button:
Done by osmosis?
No on, or off
Just an on…
And on and on to the dream
I am the witness of my thoughts
The observer of the obscene Looking all around
Seeing all but myself.
It's loud without sound
The mind's jagged edge
Tip toeing around
Left over thoughts of sewage.
What's this? Slipping and Falling
Or just falling…?
Wicked air squeezing my ears
Breath with a gurgle mid-throat
Choking on dreamed up fears
Sitting up Straight Awake!
Awake as if thrown from a boat

Eyes wide open to see
Upon the ground
As if I fell out of a tree
But in reality
So it would seem
Whatever reality is
I am awakened to the dream.

Empty Space

Too much matter
In this place
Though it is tidy the
Empty needs its space.
So pulling the plug in
The center of the room
All things drained, even emptying
Of the dustpan and broom:
Now all that is left to rid may seem absurd
It is emptier still to throw out each word.

Eternal Dream

Night winks
At the day.
Short life!
As light is severed
From multiplying darkness
A still pond taunts
A nearby brook
Now stale
Like the body
Of the departed.
Reflections
Store no information though
All gaze at it.
Into its recorder
Though nothing is kept and
The living go back and forth.
At death this stops:
Crossing over these trivialities
Nature knows the way.
And
In dreams more awake
Than conscious life is aware

That each lifetime held
In the fragilities
Of a blowing wind
Spread across the fields
Over the ages of lost time.
All of these remembered
And forgotten when the eye
Of life's final sunrise
Winks back at death's final reply
Dreams…dreams…dreams
Time and life enter eternal dreams.

False Friends

In thinking you to be a friend
You were welcomed in
But so was the end's end
Beginning with an impasse
As the face behind the mask
Could no longer hide what truth shows
As quickly as we met
The friendship now opens to a close.

Fated

A twist that you should depart
And I get to linger for
Those left behind
Get put through the ringer
Though thinking it should be
Me the one lost at sea, and
Lost in an ocean of death
You are, yet I am
The one without breath.

Flying Sea Monster

The night still asleep:
Blessed blackness bleak.
Evil skimming the waters below.
All is quiet
Within the monster's roar
(what's inside is now dead).
Rising now from the deep and
Spreading wings to soar:
Flying…
Eyes reflecting between the moon
And the water's ripples.
Lurking…
Slight jerking bleeding out
And squirting.
Left behind is the wreckage
Of a boat
Drifting…
Death's carnage a float.
Claws release bones
That drop into the ocean.

An unfortunate sailor's demise:

If found washed ashore

Enter disbelief into unsuspecting eyes.

Evil Eyes

The wind hit all
Parts of the body like
Knives puncturing a
Bag with a swimming
Gold fish: a spirit inside?
As time ran spilling
Out, so did life
Held in the grip of
Terror, and all you
Could do was watch
As life poured empty, and
All it did was stare
Blankly black.

Ageless Fun

Hide and seek was suggested
We played with our hearts invested.
Looking for you
We did
But found you not.
Hours changed to weeks:
Years collected of a sadness
No one now speaks.
With a giggle one remains in hiding
A personal lost and found is
Where you have been residing.
How do I know?
It is me in this spot
Still playing the game to avoid being caught.
(H)eide, (I)ris, (D)aren, (E)rica, and the others have grown
up
As for me I stay hid
Never aged…
Whoever finds me will find I am still a Kid.

In Place of Nothing

There will always be
The things that exist
In place of the
Things that do not.
How odd it is
To stand in for
What cannot
Exist in time
Nor place
Like a mask
Without a face.
Behind the mask
Not even a cover up
If nothing to hide.
An argument hangs around
To deafen mouths without
A thick walk in thistle
To blow the whistle
On things in place
Of that mask-less face
Taking role over empty space.

The things that exist
In place of things
That do not.

Life on the Go

Run to the forest
Get renewed, and
Hurry quick to the psychiatrist
To get unglued.
Scurry to the temple
Save the soul and
Fast…so you disassemble.
Oh, what to do
Hurry, quick
Scurry, scurry
Fast Now, hurry up
And don't be late.
Be on time
Be not left behind.
Speed up on the flash:
Surprised by the crash?

Hunger Pains

Must you surgically dissect
To understand the parts
Naked to the eye?
Like a gutted animal
Thrown on a slab.
There you are!
Guts and all…
Like spaghetti dangling
Off the sides of a rectangle.
What an unveiling
With guttural feeling
From what was a stomach
To the throat.
As if he'd just thrown up
His entire body:
"Lunch Break."

Living Inside Out

Before I leave my apartment
In the foyer I stop…
I see a smiling young
Man, I always see.
He is crippled
Yet always happy and
Happy to see me.
After our connection, I part
Leaving to catch a bus.
What I catch on the bus
Interested me much for
There was another young man.
Three seats from him
A young girl by all contrasts
Had the world by the tail
The young man's shoes:
Lace less and his face
Was on pause and
Clothes all dirty
Mindful of a lost soul
Locked up inside a body and
Constrained.

Fashioned by circumstances
I can only ponder…
Which sets my mind in wonder.
Why life houses these extremes
Of some fortunate
And some not so as it seems.
It troubles the mind and
Trembles the senses.
Of those that must live
Inside out.

Look into the Camera

Look into the camera
For it's looking into you.
Camera:
An artificial eye
With ocular lens
You see us
But pretend
Not to.
Along with ocular features
Camera!
Are you a conscious seeker?
Seeking consciousness…
Consciousness seeking
Or the finger in possession
Of such faculties.
The finger clicking
Attached to a system nervous
Of which in a symbiotic
System of semiotic
Signs.
Are we
The ones who click

With the finger
The observer of
Consciousness
Or are you?

Accused

(The blade is raised)
"Do you any last words…?"
If I profess innocence
Be it in vain
For ears will not apprentice
Nor lips if able to clear a name
At death's knock
Hollow as it is
Frail head not made of rock
Shall speak beyond its separation
Cursed chopping block
Till veneration
Opening the sentence's door
To this filth generation
Of lying tongues.

(separation)

What is innocent and true
Need not answer such question
My soul is cleared under the Heaven's blue
Sky of a penalty executed wrongly

Speaking to you frequently from beyond
About how your own life so strongly
Guilty of the execution of my mine
Will haunt you most Ghostly.
(The blade already fallen)

Love's Ending

Last kiss on the neck
As years collect into decades
You may remember to forget.
If this is true
The past still harvests
And green grass under blue
Skies of yesteryears gone
Of thoughts and memories
Seemingly living on
In you, in me
Apart forever
Where love once
Was believed to be.
Planted in true love's eternity
Its end to us both
Remains a mystery.

Mastery

Worry, Fear, and Terror
Stretching the brain, so
Left and right
Giving it a shake
I
As a wind able
To a tree
To make bare its leaves:
Worry, Fear, and Terror
Landing on the ground
worry, fear, and terror
Looking up at me
In…
worry, fear, and terror.

More to Losing His Pants

He is heard before seen
Once seen
An unveiling of the obscene.
Pushing against the wind
Shouting loudly expletives!
As his pants continuously
Give a show and
From being done up
To down they go!
Up they go!
Down they go again:
And again…
And again…
And again…
Somewhere between the
Pants being stable
And them undone
He lost his mind
In front of everyone.

Nature's Nurse

A night's
Breeze passes through a
Tree and each branch plays
The musical notes, differently.
While the leaves
In response clapped
Which encouraged the
Entire forest to continue
Its sleep aid to the
Animals in housing.

My House Is Me

My house is me
And the land that coddles it.
It is easy to see
When travelers pass
Beyond the hillside grass.
My house is really me…

My house is me.
More home than house
This is where I used to be.
Open to such buyers now.
More like you than me.

My house is still me…
My house is me can't you see?
Get out! What does die
Does now here lay
In spite of death's last say
Doesn't mean I am not here to stay.
Let me be for my house is me…

My house is your hell.
If you think it your home
Think again.
If you think this house
Is yours alone
For my house is my home.
My house is me as you will soon see…

My house is mine.
Get out get out get out.
There have been others
Over the years no doubt.
Some left in fear.
Others never made it out:
Get out! Get out! Get out!
But if your aim is to stay
Then my home is open for us to play…

My house is all alone to me.
Once again, a pinch on my soul
My new friends had to flee.
For sale sign in the grass
Once more.
As soon as they move in
I soon have them out the door.
You see…
My house is really me.

Loss

After the routine haunting
In my sleep
I zombie out of bed to collect
The fragments scattered.
Each day I put them back together…
I must
Though they crumble again
The next morning.
Make way for the spiritual leper
It is I that cometh:
Losing all my departments
Along his travel.
There are many pictures in my eyes
Portraits long ago taken from a past.
A confusion drives my sighs
Lives that seemed shorter
Than the flash.
Where have these ghosts taken up council?
What source directs back
Their wirings to me?
When asleep
They have the theatre

Of my mind in anguish and
When awake they still follow.
It matters not the dark (their garish presence is a blackhole
swallow)
Sleeping, dreaming, awakening
They continue creeping.
Their constant reaping
And all-night mind sweeping:
Falling on to the floor
Pieces of mind
Pieces of me
Falling till the end of eternity.

A Demon's Demise

Inside you are the
Full attendance
Of Satan's church.
If you lie to me from
Out of that throat
I shall cut it open
To pierce my eyes
Into your soul
To bleed out some truth
If any can be found.
I continued to slice you up
Looking for truth
Looking for life and
Found nothing
But a good try:
Well done!
Dropping to the floor
With a sigh.
Without closing the shutters
You opened up to die.
Eyes staring lifeless…

Bottomless and breathless.
Filled with the exhaustion
Of death moving in.

Wishing Well

Dividing skies are bucketing
The thirst of rain into
A weeping well of
Wishes.
A parched process in
The heat of need.
The rain continues along
With wishes that
Have been dropped
For credit.
The rain continues
Dripping and splatting
Down circular brick sinews.
The rain continues its drop
Along with coins
Destined to a hopeless
Bottom.
Costlier than the tossed
Coins that jingled
Throughout a day's melancholy
Holds a sad fact:
The wishes will never…

The rain continues its funeral.
Dead around the well
Are flowers though
In season.
While the coins continue
To be deposited
Into the well's bankruptcy
Of wishes declined.
And the faces are all
Rusted out over time.

No Escape

Jumping into the water
You got dirty. And when
You came out you
Dripped dry.
Clear as crystal
Fresh as the frankincense
Of pine needles.
Though the knifing stab of
The past's stinger has
Come out with the wash
The world is still
A forest that houses
The memory of them all.

One Breath Away

At death's depth
A lively up
Of a brand-new breath
No scarier than a hiccup
Like life before, but not
Same, yet different
Where death seemed a hovering jerk
My last breath was the perk
After a few moments of oxygen deprivation
It was the kick start needed
For an ensuing realization
End of life as it turns out
Is a yield
For I was walking a summer's field
With a loved one
Long since passed
Laughing and sharing how long it's been
As death parts
Just a breath away from things unseen
Fellow human beings inside time's watch
Fear not the keeper's score
The last breath is a short cut with a slight bend

What lies in the distance hidden?

Should not be frightened of

Nor forbidden

For there you will find tucked away in your heart

Loved ones a mere hillside apart

As you walk through summer's fields of unforgotten

To know what has died has not rotten

Their love has sought you

And your love for them which has brought you

At death's parting my friend

Walking upon summer's fields with loved ones again.

Universal Engraving

Your spirit is the splash
In ink that mimics
An exploding star that
Glows then glimmers
Without sound or light
And the universe acknowledges
And approves its
Hand-written signature.

Tips of Tress

From a distance I
Could see it in a tree…
Far away the tips
Looking at me. Blinking eye
Lashes, luscious, and lasciviously:
All this at a distance…
From the tips of a tree.

Zefla

She dances with slow rage
It slowed then
Paced, and
Then frenzied.
Then slow again
And Again…and again
Expanding and contracting.
Her rage, her breath
Which smelt of death.
She just kept dancing
Strangely sexual
At intervals
Between cycles slow
And paced
But turned ugly
In a rage.
Truth behind myth:
Died she did
At a young age.
It was suspected
Thou never proven.
The murder of those

Not far from
Her own grave.
And again
On and on
She dances with slow rage.
It was suspected
Though not proven
But what is now accepted.
On and on she dances
With a twitch
Burned she was
Zefla: the murderous witch.

The End

The End
Two words with one curtain
Could there be a new beginning afterword?
Finality put on hold to a boastful equal
When the masses love you
They push for a sequel
But part two never continues the end
When it's over twice
The same ground is covered again
Sometimes it ends at the beginning to start
While allusions mime conclusions
Polite are the doors of art
No aim to please
Just some paint and a sky
Guiding through a stories summer's breeze
Every story winds down
No matter where it starts
This is the truth of conclusion
Let us not be tempted to pretend When at first you start
It's not the beginning of THE END.

The Weight of Love

You used to love me
I loved you
Still carry it with me
Yes, it is true
The love we once
Before its end
Held together
Hand in hand
Time failed as a medicine
And losing you was scary
This love for us
I still carry.

Soul on the Run

It's just another one of those days
Wrapped up in sorrow.
A sadness that won't let go
Of yesterday's tomorrow
And I can't get free.
It was just last summer
That you and me
But not anymore.
Now
This is where I stay
Day after day
In a hotel of sadness
Where all the people
Do not know my place.
I wear this ghost town
Vacantly upon my face and
Walking with shoe laces undone
To match the weather inside
Where my soul is on the run.
Forever after has begun:
While Sitting outside cemeteries
Mourning the loss of summer fun.

Solar Birth

The womb of the Earth is
Pregnant with movement
In the belly's edge and
When fluid and still
You can at day see
The baby blue, but
At night her eyes
Shine dark.

Sliding Down

At age four
Sliding down a slide
Full of promise
Young
Reaching the bottom
Half poured out
Older
On two feet
At forty.

Silence Calling

Silence
I hear you calling
But you are too loud
So I respond by not listening.
My tummy is full, yet
My being feels empty.
Silence calling me:
You are too loud
I hear you not, and
In response
I create noise
So you
The silence
Are forced
To a whisper
Where you
Are loudest.

Side Road

The room is empty…accept
For my being locked in it.
I am not supposed to be here
I fell asleep last night
In my car parked
On the side road
In an unfamiliar
Yet safe town.
(Or so I imagined)
This room has become the alarm
That woke me
To desperation
To surroundings unknown.
Small room fit for a nursery
Perhaps…
Maybe not.
No one is in the room
To creep at me
Yet a horizontal window
In the locked door…
It stares at my vulnerability and
Chains allow for little movement.

My extremities are handcuffed and
The room is so quiet that
My ears are ringing.
The only light escaping into the room
Is let in by the slit
In the door
And something now watches.
The room is a clammy hand
On the naked part of the soul
(Without warning)
The door opens…
Light in exchange for the dark
And what spills out through
The door
Is half dead.

Shakespeare's Comedic Theme?

In the Tempest a witch
Was found unfit
Banished
By unmatched wit.

Prosperous is one
Able to undue
The problems
Of a woman shrew.

In one night's dream
In one dream's night.
Shed some light
On magical fairies' delight.

Two opposing viewpoints
Contract or not.
Hatred bleeds riches and
Your bond has let you rot.

Gender and identity
Is this the question?
If it be she
Of both worlds disguised as a he…

Shakespeare's greatest theme
As he wants us to see
Hides not under bed but
What comes out of the heart's comedy.

Plague of Death

The man with the beak mask
Just asked a question.
To me?
As his head begins to tilt with a
Voice other dimensional
Though in the same room.
Another Question?
Beak positioning
Opposite from the last and
Its shadow on the wall.
He stalks now
Then returning to a
Post of silence.
Saying more without
Words from under that beak. And
Staring without movement
In mime like essence.
Left choking on borrowed air supply
I falter and fail to reply
My head falls back to die.

Old Shoes

We put on
We take off.
Ow many shoes
To carry the weight
Of one lifetime?
Achy feet and
Smelly shoes
Traveling on highways
These stinky shoes
Walking off
The summer blues
In a breeze blown
Beyond and through
The wear and tear
Of a humid air hot
Along the travels of
A life unfair, though
Kept in tune with
Each step a little achy
Each step shaky, yet
Even though their new
My soul like shoe stench

Will be another stinky shoe
And my last new pair
When I am boxed
Goes unused seems fair.

Dreaming Dreams

Have you ever yawned
In a dream? Have you ever
Really seen what you've seen?
If it's just a dream
(Do we ever awake?)
If it's just a dream
(When awake, are we asleep?)
If it's just a dream
(Are things as they seem?)
When reality could be what
We slip in and out of
When in dreams
We zipper in and out of
Invisible seams...
It's just a dream
It's just a dream
It's just a dream
When awake we are sleeping
When sleeping we are dreaming
All states of consciousness:
Dreaming...
Dreams.

www.ingramcontent.com/pod-product-compliance
Lightning Source LLC
Chambersburg PA
CBHW071835020426
42331CB00007B/1732